ANIMAL SCAVENGERS
Vultures

SANDRA MARKLE

LERNER PUBLICATIONS COMPANY / MINNEAPOLIS

THE ANIMAL WORLD IS FULL OF SCAVENGERS.

Scavengers are the cleanup crew who find and eat carrion (dead animals) in order to survive. Every day, animals are born and animals die. Without scavengers, the bodies of dead animals would rot away slowly. The decaying flesh would smell bad and take up space. It could also pollute water and attract flies and other disease-carrying insects. Fortunately, scavengers everywhere eat dead and dying animals before they have time to rot. *In nearly every habitat, this group of scavengers includes one or more kinds of vultures.*

There are two main kinds of vultures: New World vultures and Old World vultures. New World vultures, like this lesser yellow-headed vulture, live in North, Central, and South America. They are closely related to storks. Like storks, their feet don't have sharp talons (long, sharp toenails to grab onto things). They depend on finding dead animals to eat.

Old World vultures, like these lappet-faced vultures, live in Europe, Asia, Australia, and Africa. They are closely related to hawks. Like hawks, they have sharp talons at the ends of their toes. Old World vultures occasionally kill injured animals, but they mainly scavenge for their food.

Vultures are magnificent fliers. From high in the sky, they can easily spot carrion below. Most kinds of vultures are big birds, weighing as much as 30 pounds (about 14 kilograms). They have huge wings that stretch nearly 6 feet (about 2 meters) from wing tip to wing tip. But it isn't only wing size that makes vultures such good fliers. These birds can glide great distances using naturally rising air currents.

It's early morning on the African savanna (grassland). The white-backed vultures are stirring. High in an old dead tree, the male white-backed starts to spread his wings. When he feels a thermal, or warm air current flowing up from the ground, he flaps his big wings and rides the rising air current. Then he glides effortlessly, while watching for carrion on the ground below.

Vultures have extremely sharp eyesight.
The male white-backed sees other vultures circling in the distance. This
means that carrion is below on the ground. He glides closer and then
drops, thrusting out his legs just in time for touchdown.

Other vultures are already feeding on the dead animal. The male white-backed hurries to grab his share. His sharp-tipped beak is made of the same sturdy material as human fingernails, only thicker. He uses his beak to pull off the bits of flesh he gulps down.

Suddenly, a scavenging jackal charges into the group of feeding vultures. The male white-backed flaps and lifts off. He hurries to get out of the jackal's way. He doesn't want to risk harming his big fragile wings by defending his share of the meal. But the jackal isn't looking for a fight. As soon as it grabs a meaty bone, it trots away with its prize. Then the white-backed settles down to feed some more.

A vulture doesn't sing or call the way most birds do. It hisses, wheezes, and makes cackling noises as it forces air from its lungs. Feeding vultures make lots of noise as they struggle with each other to get to the carrion. They stick their long necks inside the carcass in search of the juiciest bits.

In less than ten minutes, the male's crop (the food storage sack inside his body) is so full his chest is bulging. Too heavy to fly, he sits drowsily. He watches the other vultures eat until there is nothing left but a bony skeleton.

In the vulture's stomach, strong acid mixes with the food as part of the digestive process. The food vultures eat is often rotting and disease-infected. But few viruses or bacteria can survive in this bird's stomach. A vulture's blood is packed with antibodies. These disease-fighting molecules will attack any bacteria that survive his stomach.

The male white-backed vulture's head is bloody from reaching into the carcass. He heads off to the river for a good wash.

After his wash, the male white-backed vulture preens his wings as they dry. He pulls his feathers, one at a time, through his beak to ready his wings for flight. Feathers are made up of many small branches held together by tiny hooks. Flying and brushing against carrion or other birds unhook the feathers' branches. Preening zips them up again.

Suddenly, an elephant charges toward the water. Running and flapping hard, all the male white-backed vultures lift off in time to escape. Then the male heads home to the tall tree he left that morning.

Far away along the Gulf Coast of Florida, dozens of turkey vultures share one dead tree. Nearly every branch is occupied. These turkey vultures, like other New World vultures, have feet with toes pointing forward. These toes allow the birds to stand and walk but not to grab things. Old World vultures have a hind toe that they can use like a thumb for grabbing.

Turkey vultures gather in communal (group) roosts. Near the roost, a mated pair makes a nest in an opening within a dense thicket. Here the female turkey vulture lays two oval, creamy white and brown spotted eggs. Each is about as big as an adult human's hand. Then, for about forty days, the parents take turns—one day on and one day off—sitting on the eggs to keep them warm while the chicks develop.

After they hatch, the chicks can't regulate their body temperature at first. The parents have to sit on the nest to keep the chicks warm. They also have to find food for them. One chick dies, even though the parents did all they could to keep it alive. Both parents still work hard to find food and bring it home to their surviving chick.

A few vultures, such as turkey vultures, have an excellent sense of smell. The female turkey vulture flies low over the dense forest. She can tell as much from what she smells in the air currents as from what she sees below. Many of the animals that turkey vultures eat die in forests and are hidden by trees. Being able to smell carrion helps vultures locate food they can't see. Other kinds of vultures, such as black vultures, often watch for circling turkey vultures to find a meal.

The female turkey vulture tracks the scent of carrion to its source, a dead alligator. A black vulture has already claimed it. Hissing, the black vulture warns the turkey vulture to stay away.

Finally, the female turkey vulture finds another food source, dead fish on a riverbank. She lands and immediately begins to feed.

Meanwhile, a raccoon out hunting for its own meal detects the strong scent of the turkey vulture chick.

Then the chick smells the hunter and exhales forcefully. This makes a loud, roaring hiss. It's enough to drive the raccoon away, and the chick is safe.

In a jungle in Peru, a male king vulture searches for a meal to feed his chick. The king vulture doesn't have a good sense of smell. But he does have sharp eyesight. When he spots black vultures on a riverbank, he swoops down to investigate. The black vultures are eating rotting fish.

The black vultures don't give up their food without a squabble. The more aggressive king vulture hisses and nips at them. Finally, he's able to grab a share of this meal.

Still not full, the king vulture flies off in search of more food. This time, he finds a dead horse. Because the horse's skin is tough, the vulture eats the eyes and other soft bits first. When other vultures arrive to help nip open the belly, he fights for his share of the soft parts inside.

At last, he's eaten enough to carry food home to his chick. In fact, his crop is so full it's bulging. He has to run and flap hard to get airborne.

Both parents bring home food to the young female king vulture.
She grows bigger quickly. Her wings become stronger. She sheds her down for the dark feathers of a juvenile vulture. Although she's inside a small nest cavity in a tall tree, she still opens and closes her wings to strengthen them. Finally, she's able to fly away to search for her own meals.

For about nine months, the juvenile king vulture is a scavenger in training. She tags along after her parents and learns by watching and copying their actions. This is how she learns to spot other vultures in the air or on the ground. She learns to follow them to find carrion. She also learns to fight to get her share away from competitors.

By the time the young female king vulture has her adult feathers, she's a skilled scavenger. She also has a mate and has claimed a cavity in the top of a tree for a nest. She carries food home in her bulging crop to feed her single chick. Another chick will grow up to join the world's vulture cleanup crew.

Looking Back

- Look again at the vulture in flight on the title page (page 1). Then look at the vulture on page 9. See how the bird has changed the position of its neck and tail in order to slow down and come in for a landing. A vulture also changes the position of its tail, using it like a rudder, to change direction while flying.

- Take another look at the vultures eating on page 12. Did you guess how the fluffy feather collar helps them? It keeps blood from running down their backs and onto their wings while they're eating. If their wing feathers were matted and weighted down with blood, they could have trouble taking flight to escape a predator.

- Look at the turkey vulture chick on page 27. How is this youngster like the adult turkey vulture on page 20? How will it change as it grows up?

Glossary

ANTIBODIES: disease-fighting molecules found in the blood

BEAK: the body part around the vulture's mouth

CARRION: a dead animal that a scavenger eats

CHICK: a baby bird

CROP: a sacklike part of a bird's digestive track where food is stored

DIGESTIVE PROCESS: the process of eating and the breakdown of food in the body for energy

JUVENILE: a young adult vulture. The feathers of juveniles are not the same color as the feathers of older adults.

PREEN: to clean and groom feathers

ROOST: a place, such as a tree or manmade structure, where vultures rest

SCAVENGER: an animal that feeds on dead animals

THERMAL: a rising current of warm air produced when the sun's heat energy warms the land, which heats the air above it

Further Information

Books

Grady, Wayne. *Vulture: Nature's Ghastly Gourmet.* San Francisco: Sierra Club Books, 1997. This book examines the myths and real life histories of vultures.

Rauzon, Mark. *Vultures.* New York: Franklin Watts, 1997. This book describes the physical characteristics, behavior, and life cycles of various species of vultures.

Redmond, Jim. *King Vulture.* Chicago: Raintree/Steck Vaughn, 2003. This is an account of the life cycle and special behavior of king vultures.

Smith, Roland. *Vultures.* Minneapolis: Lerner Publications Company, 1997. This photo essay presents various types of vultures and describes their behavior and life cycle.

Wechsler, Doug. *Vultures.* New York: Rosen, 2003. This book tells about Old and New World vultures.

Video

Wings over the Serengeti (Washington, DC: National Geographic, 1996). This film dramatically depicts the food chain on Africa's Serengeti, including scavengers such as vultures.

Website

The Turkey Vulture Society. http://vulturesociety. homestead.com. Find questions and answers about turkey vultures and other vultures.

Index

air currents, 6, 8, 22
alligator, 24

bacteria, 14
beak, 10, 30
black vulture, 22, 24, 28
blood, 14

carrion, 2, 4, 6, 8, 9, 12, 14, 17, 22, 35
chick, 20, 21, 26, 27, 28, 31, 32, 36
communal roost, 20
crop, 13, 31, 36

eating, 10, 12, 13, 14, 25
eggs, 20
eyes, 9, 22, 28

feathers, 17, 36
flight, 6, 8, 9, 10, 17, 20, 28, 30, 31, 32

jackal, 10

king vulture, 28, 30, 31, 32, 35, 36

lappet-faced vulture, 5
lesser yellow-headed vulture, 4

mated pair, 20

neck, 12
nest, 20, 32, 36
New World vultures, 4, 18

Old World vultures, 4, 5, 18

predators, 26, 27
preening, 17
prey, 5

raccoon, 26, 27

savanna, 8
scavengers, 2, 4, 5, 9, 10, 35, 36
sense of smell, 22, 24, 26, 28
sounds, 12, 24, 27, 28
stomach, 14

talons (and feet), 4, 5, 18
thermal, 8
turkey vulture, 18, 20, 21, 22, 24, 25, 26

white-backed vultures, 8, 9, 10, 13, 14, 17
wings, 6, 10, 17, 32

With special appreciation for Dr. Jonathan Pascoe

The author would like to thank the following people for sharing their expertise and enthusiasm: Dr. David Houston, Environmental and Evolutionary Biology, University of Glasgow, Glasgow, Scotland; and Dr. Jerome A. Jackson, Whitaker Eminent Scholar at Florida Gulf Coast University, Fort Meyers, Florida. The author would also like to express a special thank-you to Skip Jeffery for his help and support during the creative process.

Photo Acknowledgments

The images in this book are used with the permission of: © Peter Blackwell/ naturepl.com, p. 1; © Craig Lovell/CORBIS, p. 3; © Mark Jones/Roving Tortoise Photos, p. 4; © Wendy Stone/CORBIS, p. 5; © Joe McDonald/CORBIS, pp. 7, 19; © D. Robert & Lorri Franz/CORBIS, p. 8; © Richard DuToit/naturepl.com, p. 9; © Tony Heald/naturepl.com, pp. 11, 16; © danheller.com, p. 12; © M. P. Kahl/ VIREO, p. 13; © Paul A. Souders/ CORBIS, p. 15; © Peter Johnson/ CORBIS, p. 20; © Frans Lanting/ Minden Pictures, p. 21; © A. Morris/VIREO, pp. 23, 25; © Doug Wechsler/ VIREO, p. 24; © Raymond Gehman/ CORBIS, p. 26; © Rick Kline/ Cornell Lab of Ornithology, p. 27; © Tui De Roy/Roving Tortoise Photos, pp. 29, 30, 31; © Brand X Pictures by Getty Images, p. 33; © Mark Jones/Roving Tortoise Photos, pp. 34, 37. Front cover: © Chris Hellier/CORBIS. Back cover (top): © Joe McDonald/CORBIS. Back cover (bottom): *Army Ants:* © Christian Ziegler; *Hyenas:* © Richard du Toit/naturepl.com; *Jackals:* © Beverly Joubert/National Geographic/Getty Images; *Tasmanian Devils:* Photodisc Royalty Free by Getty Images; *Vultures:* © Chris Hellier/CORBIS; *Wolverines:* © Daniel J. Cox/naturalexposures.com.

Lerner Publications Company
A division of Lerner Publishing Group
241 First Avenue North
Minneapolis, MN 55401

Website address: www.lernerbooks.com

Library of Congress Cataloging-in-Publication Data

Markle, Sandra.
  Vultures / by Sandra Markle.
    p.   cm. — (Animal scavengers)
  Includes bibliographical references and index.
  ISBN-13: 978−0−8225−3195−1 (lib. bdg. : alk. paper)
  ISBN-10: 0−8225−3195−X (lib. bdg. : alk. paper)
  1. Vultures—Juvenile literature. I. Title. II. Series: Markle, Sandra. Animal scavengers.
QL696.F32M258 2005
598.9'2—dc22   2004029669

Manufactured in the United States of America
1 2 3 4 5 6 − DP − 10 09 08 07 06 05

READ ANIMAL PREDATORS, A *BOOKLIST* TOP 10 YOUTH NONFICTION SERIES BY SANDRA MARKLE

Crocodiles
Great White Sharks
Killer Whales
Lions
Owls
Polar Bears
Wolves